NEIL T. ANDERSON

THE
BONDAGE
BREAKER®
STUDY GUIDE

HARVEST HOUSE PUBLISHERS
EUGENE, OREGON

Cover by Dugan Design Group, Bloomington, Minnesota

Cover photo © istockphoto/abzee

THE BONDAGE BREAKER® STUDY GUIDE
Copyright © 1992, 1993, 2000 by Harvest House Publishers
Eugene, Oregon 97408
www.harvesthousepublishers.com

ISBN 978-0-7369-2059-9 (pbk.)
ISBN 978-0-7369-3129-8 (eBook)

Printed in the United States of America

17 18 19 / BP / 15 14 13 12

Contents

Abundant Life Through Jesus Christ,
the Bondage Breaker   5

Part One: Take Courage!

1. You Don't Have to Live in the Shadows   9
2. Finding Your Way in the World 17
3. You Have Every Right to Be Free 27
4. You Can Win the Battle for Your Mind 35
5. Confronting the Rebel Prince 41
6. Jesus Has You Covered 49

Part Two: Stand Firm!

7. Manipulating Spirits 59
8. The Lure of Knowledge and Power 65
9. Tempted to Do It Your Way 71
10. Accused by the Father of Lies 79
11. The Danger of Deception 85
12. The Danger of Losing Control 95

Part Three: Walk Free!

13. Steps to Freedom in Christ 103
14. Helping Others Find Freedom in Christ 133

A Final Encouragement 141

Abundant Life Through Jesus Christ, The Bondage Breaker

*"I came that they might have life,
and might have it abundantly."*
—John 10:10

Those words were spoken by Jesus Christ, the Good Shepherd. He gave His life for us, His sheep, so that we might experience life abundantly and life eternal. But for too many believers the words of that promise sound empty, and the reality seems far away.

Do the words of Jesus' promise sound empty to you? Do you feel far away from the joy and peace that other Christians seem to experience? Instead of enjoying a productive life of freedom in Jesus Christ, do you seem to be in bondage to fear, anger, or depression? Are you struggling with habits you can't break, thoughts or inner voices you can't silence, or sinful behavior you can't escape?

It's for people like you that I've written *The Bondage Breaker* and this study guide. *The Bondage Breaker* explains your position of life, freedom, protection, and authority in Christ. It warns of your vulnerability to very real demonic influences that are intent on robbing you of your freedom, and tells you of your need to submit to God and resist the devil. The book also presents the Steps to Freedom in Christ, which will help you walk free of the enemy's designs on your life.

But simply reading about these things is quite different from living out the freedom that Jesus desires you to have, and that's why I've written this guide—to help you apply to your own life what you read about in *The Bondage Breaker*. I encourage you to work through this book slowly and thoroughly and to pray each step of the way.

As you work through these lessons, you'll be studying more closely the Scriptures I refer to in the text; taking a closer look at your own life, past and present; and, I pray, opening yourself to the work of God in your life. Linger over the passages of Scripture. Let God speak to your heart and use His Word to work in your life. May this be an opportunity for you to draw closer to your loving and powerful heavenly Father.

It is also my prayer that you will be able to personalize the Bible's powerful words of truth, believe its life-changing message of hope, and experience the freedom and abundant life which are available to you through the work of Jesus Christ, your Shepherd and your Bondage Breaker.

—Neil Anderson

Part One

Take Courage!

You Don't Have to Live in the Shadows

CHAPTER 1

Are You Living in the Shadows?

Dear God,

> Where are you? How can you watch and not help me? I
> hurt so bad, and you don't even care....I love you, but you
> seem so far away. I can't hear you or feel you or see you, but
> I'm supposed to believe you're here...

Perhaps you can identify with this woman's feelings. Perhaps you've felt this way in the past or are feeling this way now. The message of this chapter—and this book—is that you don't have to live in the shadows.

- Why are you reading *The Bondage Breaker* and working through this study guide? What do you hope to learn about God's ability to work in your life and His power over Satan?

• Read again the following passage from page 18:

> Many other Christians I deal with don't complain about hearing voices as such, but their minds are filled with such confusion that their daily walk with Christ is unfulfilling and unproductive. When they try to pray, they begin thinking about a million other things they should be doing. When they sit down to read the Bible or a good Christian book, they can't concentrate, or they read for several minutes and suddenly realize that their thoughts have been a million miles away. When they have an opportunity to serve the Lord in some way, they are brought up short by discouraging thoughts of self-doubt: "I'm not a strong Christian"; "I don't know enough about the Bible"; "I'm still plagued by sinful thoughts"; or "I don't have many spiritual gifts." Instead of being victorious, productive, joy-filled Christians, they trudge through life under a cloud, just trying to hang on until Jesus comes. Some of this is certainly because of lack of mental discipline and patterns of the flesh, but it can also reflect deception from the enemy. I have seen thousands of people freed from this kind of mental torment.

Where, if at all, do you see yourself in this description? Where might the enemy be deceiving you or robbing you of the joy of the Christian life?

• Define "bondage" in your own words.

— What do you feel when you hear that word?

Common Misconceptions About Bondage

• There is much confusion about the presence and activity of demons in the world today. This confusion keeps many

Christians in bondage to a power they don't acknowledge. After reading pages 19–26, write out in your own words arguments against the following misconceptions about the spiritual world.

1. Demons were active when Christ was on earth, but their activity has subsided today.

2. What the early church called demonic activity we now understand to be mental illness.

3. Some problems are psychological and some are spiritual.

4. Christians aren't subject to demon activity.

5. Demonic influence is only evident in extreme or violent behavior and gross sin.

6. Freedom from spiritual bondage is the result of a power encounter with demonic forces.

• Which misconception(s) have you accepted as truth? Rebut that idea with a passage from Scripture that refers to God's power, His truth, or Satan's defeat. Write that verse out here and on an index card to carry with you to remind you of your victory over Satan through Christ.

Know the Enemy and the Victor

- Look up the following passages. Write down the phrases used to describe Satan.

— John 8:44

— John 10:10

— 1 John 5:19

— Revelation 12:9

- Compare those terms for Satan with the following descriptions of Jesus and His Holy Spirit.

— John 6:48

— John 14:6

— John 16:13

— Isaiah 9:6

The Armor of God

• Read Ephesians 6:12 and 2 Corinthians 10:3-5. Note the present-tense verbs. What is Paul saying about what believers will encounter in this world?

• Believers are not left defenseless in the face of the enemy. Read Ephesians 6:10-18.

— List the six components of the "full armor of God." (We'll look at them more closely in Chapter 6.)

— When should we be praying?

— What does the role of prayer suggest about the nature of spiritual warfare?

Setting Captives Free

• Why is there so little instruction on "setting captives free" in the epistles? Look again at the section in which I point to the cross, and give two reasons. Read the scriptural support, and explain the reasons in your own words.

— Matthew 28:18 and Colossians 2:15

— Ephesians 1:18-21 and 2:4-7

- When one woman was experiencing deep spiritual, mental, and emotional turmoil, she wrote the letter to God quoted at the beginning of the chapter. Take time now to write to God. Cry to Him for help. Share what's on your heart. Ask Him to work in your life.

— If you can—and you may not be able to now—write a letter from God in response to your letter to Him. In it, personalize verses from the Bible. Let God address you specifically through His Word by weaving your name into the text you choose.

— Maybe at this point in your journey, the darkness is too thick for you to imagine God saying anything to you. If so, read the letter to the Lost Sheep on page 28, and replace "Lost Sheep" with your name.

The Truth Shall Set You Free

- The truth of God's love and His power is what liberates Christians from the hold of the enemy. Which of the following verses, or which verse of your own choosing, is an especially effective reminder of that fact? Write it out here. (You might also want to write it on an index card to carry with you or to put in a strategic place where it can remind you of God's power over evil, confusion, and despair.)

— John 14:6

— John 17:15,17

— Philippians 4:8

— Romans 8:38,39

— 1 Peter 3:21,22

• After reading this chapter, what new truth have you realized, or what truth are you now seeing more clearly?

• Spend a few minutes with the Lord. Share your letter with Him, and listen for His quiet response. Share your fears and doubts with your heavenly Father, your almighty King. The prayer "I do believe; help my unbelief" (Mark 9:24) has proven effective for many saints through the centuries.

Finding Your Way in the World

CHAPTER 2

The Devil at Work

• How is the deceiver at work in the world today?

— What is the enemy doing through "the rise of the New Age movement, the acceptance of parapsychology as a science, the growing popularity of the supernatural, and the increasing visibility of Satanism in our culture" (page 29)?

• What warning should believers and nonbelievers alike take from this understanding of the deceiver's present-day working?

The Two-Tier Worldview

• What is the basic difference between the Western worldview and the Eastern worldview?

• What is the biblical reality about the relationship between the natural and the spiritual or supernatural?

• What do the following passages suggest about the supernatural?

— Ephesians 6:10-12

— Romans 8:38,39

— 1 Peter 3:22

— Colossians 1:16

— 1 Corinthians 10:20,21

• Why must we who are Christians include the kingdom of darkness in our worldview?

• Dee had developed physical symptoms which were diag-
nosed as multiple sclerosis. After she renounced her request
for a thorn in the flesh and prayed to be freed from any
influence by Satan in her life, the symptoms disappeared.
Most doctors and psychologists would not even consider
Dee's condition to be a spiritual problem.

— Why do many believers today, along with doctors and
psychologists, tend not to consider the possibility of spiritual causes for physical ailments?

— What is the result of not considering the possible spiritual basis for physical problems?

Living in the Excluded Middle

• Scripture teaches that supernatural, spiritual forces are at
work in the world. What do the following passages teach or
illustrate about those forces?

— Mark 5:1-20

— Luke 4:33-37

— Luke 13:11,12

— 1 John 3:8

— Hebrews 2:14

- "I am convinced that many Christians battle physical symptoms unsuccessfully through natural means when the essence of the problem and the solution is psychological and spiritual" (page 34).

  — What questions does this statement raise for you?

  — Do you agree with the statement? Why or why not?

Getting Spiritual without God

- "The center of the secular worldview is self: What will *I* get out of this? Who will meet *my* needs? I'm doing *my own* thing. Even a Christian who operates in this sphere is motivated by selfish ambition and pride" (page 35).

  — Why is self such a powerful tool for Satan to use?

  — Why are selfish ambition and pride effective weapons for Satan to use against the kingdom of God?

- Look at Matthew 16:13-16,21-23.

  — What does Peter confidently proclaim in verses 13-16?

— What news does he react to in verse 22?

— Why is this reaction satanic in principle? In other words, what motivates Peter to say what he does?

The View from the Cross

• How is a situation where people "are their own gods" a logical extension of self-interest?

• Why is being one's own god so appealing?

• And why is being one's own god so wrong?

• Where does being one's own god lead?

• Turn to Genesis chapters 2 and 3, the account of Adam and Eve in the garden of Eden.

— What does God command in Genesis 2:15-17?

— How does the serpent (and Eve herself!) twist those words in Genesis 3:1-5?

• Why don't human beings succeed at being their own gods?

• Look at what Jesus teaches His disciples in Matthew 16:24-27. Why is obedience to this teaching crucial to a healthy spiritual life?

Jesus' words in Matthew 16:24-27 offer six guidelines for freedom from bondage to the world system and the devil who inspires that bondage.

Deny Yourself

• How is denying yourself different from self-denial?

• What do you do when you deny yourself?

• Why is denying oneself essential to spiritual freedom?

Pick Up Your Cross Daily

• What has the cross of Christ provided for believers?

• What do the following Scriptures teach about who we are because of Jesus' death on the cross?

— 1 Peter 1:18,19

— 1 John 3:1-3

— Colossians 3:4

• What does the phrase "pick up your cross" mean to you?

• How does the command to pick up your cross counter Satan's invitation to be your own god?

Follow Christ

• Where will Christ lead you if you follow Him?

• What benefits come from following Christ? Let the following Scriptures serve as a starting point for your list.

— John 10:27,28

— Romans 8:14

— Romans 12:2

—

—

Sacrifice the Lower Life to Gain the Higher Life

• Jesus says, "Everyone who has left houses or brothers or sisters or father or mother or children or farms for My name's sake shall receive many times as much, and shall inherit eternal life" (Matthew 19:29). What does this statement teach about what is truly valuable?

• How can pursuing the things of the world keep you from pursuing and attaining spiritual things?

• What does 1 Timothy 4:8 say about what is worth pursuing?

Sacrifice the Pleasure of Things to Gain the Pleasure of Life

• Look around. What lasting pleasures does the world offer?

• Now look at Galatians 5:22,23. What blessings or fruits does the Holy Spirit offer?

• What does your checkbook reflect about which you are pursuing—the pleasures of the world or the blessings of the Spirit?

• Read Luke 10:38-42.

— What is Martha interested in? And Mary?

— Are you more like Martha or Mary?

— How is this passage encouraging you or convicting you?

Sacrifice the Temporal to Gain the Eternal

• According to Hebrews 11:24-26, how does Moses illustrate the principle of sacrificing the temporal to gain the eternal?

• How have you sacrificed the temporal to gain the eternal?

A Look at Yourself

• Complete the following chart:

Satan's ultimate lie:_____

Christ's ultimate truth:_____

Satan's ultimate bond: _____

Christ's ultimate freedom: _____

• How are you living independently of God right now?

— Confess those areas where you have been in charge, and relinquish control to Christ.

— Ask God to show you those areas where you are lord but which you don't see.

— Ask God to forgive you for usurping His rightful place as Lord of every area of your life.

— Renew your commitment to live with Jesus as Lord of your life.

You Have Every Right to Be Free

CHAPTER 3

How Do You Perceive Yourself?

- Just as I asked Lydia, I want to ask you how you perceive yourself. Be as specific as possible (are you good? evil? somewhere in between?), and then consider how well your perceptions line up with the truth of Scripture.

- Look at the list of Scriptures that tell us who we are "in Christ" on pages 43–45.

  — Read aloud these biblical statements of affirmation.

  — Choose one or two passages to memorize as a reminder of who you are in Christ.

- Why would Satan want to convince you that you are worthless and evil?

The following concepts are foundational to your freedom from spiritual conflict as a child of God and are foundational to freedom from Satan's efforts to convince you that you are worthless and evil. Look up the supporting Scriptures and summarize what they say about the concepts listed below. And remember that when we find a promise in the Bible, we claim it. When we come to a commandment, we obey it. But when we read a truth, we believe it. Believe these words of truth as you meditate on them!

You Are a Child of God

— 1 John 3:1-3 (What is our relationship to God the Father, based on what He has done? What is our hope now?)

— John 1:12 (What has God given to us?)

— Romans 8:16,17 (Who is it that affirms our place before God?)

• Think again about being a child of God. How will believing this about yourself affect your life?

• Pick out two or three reasons why understanding and affirming who we are in Christ is so important.

You Are Spiritually and Therefore Eternally Alive

— Ephesians 1:1-13, especially verses 7 and 13. (What is our standing in relation to Christ once we accept Him as Savior and Lord?)

— 1 Corinthians 6:19,20. (Who lives in you?)

— Romans 8:9-11. (What promise do you find here?)

• How can you dispute Satan's accusation that you are not spiritually and therefore eternally alive?

• Look at 1 John 4:11,12. When have you "seen God" in the love of His people? Be specific.

You Are a New Creation in Christ

— Romans 5:8-11. (Why can you rejoice?)

— Ephesians 2:1-5. (How were you saved from your sins?)

— Colossians 1:13,14,22. (Describe the new creation you are in Christ.)

• How can Satan use the thought that we are only "sinners saved by grace" to bind us?

• What word does the Scripture use to describe your actual status? (See Colossians 1:12.) What reassurance does that word give you?

— Romans 6:6,7. (What action is Paul talking about here?)

• Look again at the list of Scripture verses on pages 43–45, and list out for yourself some of the things we have gained through being identified with Christ.

• How are your thoughts, words, and actions different since you became a believer? How does your behavior reflect the truth that you are a new creature in Christ (2 Corinthians 5:17)?

You Can Be Victorious over Sin and Death

Let the discussion on pages 53–57 help you grasp the meaning of Romans 6, and then summarize its major points by answering the questions below.

— Romans 6:1-11. (What relationship with sin did God allow Jesus to have? Why?)

— Romans 6:12,13. (How are believers to relate to sin now?)

— Romans 12:1. (What choice does every believer have?)

• What—and whose—experience is necessary for you to be dead to sin? (See pages 50,51.) Praise God for that truth!

• Why is Romans 12:1 important to someone who wants to be victorious over sin and the flesh? What does it say about that person's role in the victory?

You Can Be Free from the Power of Sin

Walk slowly through my discussion with Dan on pages 53–57.

— Romans 7:15-17. (How many players are there? Identify them.)

— Romans 7:18-21. (Which player is bad? Why is that good news for Dan and you?)

— Romans 7:22-25. (Where does the battle rage? What is inflicting the pain? Who is the source of victory?)

• Where do you most identify with Dan (and the apostle Paul)?

• What words from my discussion with Dan offer you new insight and hope?

A Look Back...

• Which of the five foundational truths discussed in this chapter speaks most directly to your present situation?

• What comfort, encouragement, and correction did the discussion of these truths offer you?

• What new truth did you discover in this chapter, or what familiar truth did you hear as if for the first time?

And a Look at Yourself

• How could your actions more clearly reflect your belief that you are the dearly loved and accepted child of God? What can you do to better live like a child of God? Be specific.

- What passages of Scripture referred to in this chapter are particularly helpful to you today in those areas in which you are in bondage? Choose one to commit to memory, and begin working on that passage today.

- Spend some time with the Lord, thanking Him for the freedom He offers His children. Ask God to help you counter with His powerful truth the doubts that Satan sows; to let go of your debilitating self-image as a sinner; to more clearly reflect that you are a new creature in Christ so you can be light in this dark world; and to free you from raging against yourself in your struggle with sin. Thank God, too, for the fact that victory is truly available through Jesus Christ our Lord!

You Can Win
the Battle for Your Mind

CHAPTER 4

Think About Your Own Battle

In chapter 3, Dan and I had a conversation about the struggle in his mind over his feelings about who he was. As we read through the Scripture from Romans 7, he began to see himself in a new light.

He was asking the same question that so many believers have: "If the Scriptures about who I am in Christ are true, then how come I still struggle with the same thoughts and feelings I did before I became a Christian?"

• Have you wrestled with this question yourself? Think about it again (or for the first time) before you go on.

— What is Paul's exhortation to believers in regard to their minds?

— Why is this so important?

— In Romans 12:2, who do you think is doing the transforming?

— How does this help us with our feelings?

Strongholds of Self-Defense

• How are defense mechanisms similar to "strongholds" ("fortresses")?

— What is the answer to our problem with strongholds?

— How can we "unlearn" them?

Satan's Schemes

• What is Satan's aim in the battle for our minds?

• Paul expresses his concern for the Corinthians in 2 Corinthians 10:5; 2:10,11; and 11:3 (pages 61,62). How can

Satan's schemes damage our relationships with others, especially other believers?

• "After helping thousands [of people] find their freedom in Christ, I can testify that unforgiveness is the major reason people remain in bondage to the past" (page 62). The "Steps" in chapter 13 deal with forgiveness more extensively, but try to list right now two or three areas in which the Holy Spirit may be prompting you to exercise forgiveness towards other people.

Satan and Our Minds

• With your Bible open to Genesis 3:1-13 (the account of the fall of Adam and Eve), consider Satan's strategies in the lives of David, Judas, and Ananias and Sapphira. How do these strategies relate to the original lie?

— What does this also tell you about the type of thoughts Satan will try to put in your mind?

— Does it help you to know that many other believers have experienced Satan's deceptions in their thoughts? Why?

"Not Against Flesh and Blood"

• Go back to the first part of chapter 1, "You Don't Have to Live in the Shadows," in the book (pages 17,18) and reread it. Do you view this woman's experience differently after reading "Not Against Flesh and Blood" (pages 65,66)? Why or why not?

— What would you say to her about her inner conflict?

• The struggle of the believer is "not against flesh and blood." What are some of the ways we can try to "explain this away"?

Brain vs. Mind

• Why is the illustration about computer hardware and software helpful in understanding demonic spiritual influence?

• It's important to be able to distinguish between normal dreams and demonically influenced dreams. How can we make this evaluation?

• Read Psalm 119:147,148. What strategy does this suggest to you to combat deceptive and discouraging thoughts that come at night?

The Battle Is Real

• People often say to each other, "It's all in your own mind," meaning that something doesn't really exist at all. What have you learned that might make you respond to someone differently?

• In the story of the frightened child, what does the parent do to reassure the child?

— How would you apply this to your own life?

• Look again at the experiences of various people which I describe (pages 69–71). What is it that is critical to help people to enjoy quietness and freedom in Christ?

Taking Every Thought Captive

• Why, in one sense, does it not make any difference to us where lying or condemning thoughts come from?

• What promise does God give us in regard to our prayers? (See Philippians 4:7.)

• Why does our rebelliousness in being bitter and unforgiving cause so much damage? (See James 4:6.)

Postscript: Freedom Is Available

• Which defense mechanisms (see pages 60, 61) do you think are present in your own life?

— How do you now see that God can give (or is giving) you victory in these areas?

• List some Scripture verses from this chapter that can help you be victorious in the battle for your mind. Put two or three of these on a card to carry with you and remind yourself of the availability of victory.

• Turn to Philippians 4:4-9. Write out the commands to be obeyed and the promises to be claimed. Think about how the commands and promises relate to the battle for your mind. Spend some time asking God to open your eyes to your life and position in Christ that make your understanding and obedience possible. Thank God also for making freedom available to you through His son.

Confronting
the Rebel Prince
CHAPTER 5

Carrying Jesus' Badge of Authority

Before we discuss in detail the reality and present activity of Satan and his demons, you need to understand your position of authority in Christ as it relates to the spiritual realm.

• Your resistance of the devil is based on the authority you possess in Christ.

— The disciples' resistance of the devil was based on the authority they possessed in Christ. In Luke 10:17, they acknowledged this authority as they rejoiced over the results of their ministry. What was crucial to their success?

— The disciples were spiritually in tune enough to know that demons existed and were a force to be reckoned with. Why do you think that today fewer followers of Christ acknowledge the reality of demons?

• Turn to Luke 10:19,20. What was and is to be the main priority of people who want to heal and release people from the bondage of demons?

• What part does our position in Christ play in our authority over the kingdom of darkness?

• Look at Matthew 4:3,4. On whom does Jesus depend in His resistance of the devil? On whom are we to depend?

The Right and the Ability to Rule

It is *truth* which sets you free, not the knowledge of error. You would have no authority at all if it weren't for your identity as a child of God and your position in Christ. *Who you are* must always take precedence over *what you do*.

• Jesus gave His disciples both authority and power over demons.

— What is authority?

— What is power?

— Why do Jesus' disciples need both authority and power?

- What lesson does the story of David and Goliath teach you about your ability to resist Satan and his demons? (See 1 Samuel 17 and pages 78,79.)

- What is the basis for success in finding our freedom in Christ and helping others to do the same? (It's not education, calling, or personality!)

Pulling Rank

- Too often spiritual warfare involving God, Satan, and you and me is viewed as a tug-of-war on a horizontal plane, but this picture is not right. What is the biblical and therefore correct view? (Matthew 28:18, Romans 13:1, and Luke 10:17 will help you answer this question.)

- According to the text, why does the kingdom of darkness exert such negative influence in the world and in the lives of Christians?

- As we saw in the preceding chapter, what we believe affects how we act. How do our beliefs about our authority in the spiritual realm affect our actions?

- What does 1 John 5:18 promise believers?

• What should our response be when the enemy tries to incite fear in us?

The Riches of Our Inheritance in Christ

Do you and I enjoy the same claim to Christ's authority in the spiritual realm as those who were personally sent out by Him? Yes!

• How is our position even more advantageous than that of the early disciples? Compare Mark 3:14,15 (the "then" picture) with Ephesians 1:3-13 (the "now" picture).

• Paul prayed that the believers' inner eyes would be opened. What did he want the Christians at Ephesus, and us today, to see?

• How can our blindness prevent us from exercising the authority of Christ in our lives?

The Depth and Breadth of Authority

• According to Ephesians 1:19-23, what is the power source for the authority we have in Christ?

• How does Paul identify the expanse of Christ's authority?

• In which realm is this tremendous authority in Christ active through us?

Authority Conferred

The moment you receive Christ, you are seated with Him in the heavenlies. Your identity as a child of God and your authority over spiritual powers are things you have *right now.*

• Open your Bible to Ephesians 1 and 2.

— What was God's supreme act of power and authority? (See 1:19-21.)

— According to 2:4-6, what did God do for you and me?

• The resurrection of Christ from the tomb and our resurrection from spiritual death happened at the same time. Look at Colossians 2:15. What happened to Satan at that moment?

• Despite the facts outlined in Ephesians and Colossians, many believers fail to experience victory in their lives. By what means is Satan able to introduce defeat into the lives of Christians?

• How do you react to these facts about the depth and breadth of the authority available to you in Jesus Christ? What rethinking does this cause you to do about the world situation? About believers who are held in bondage by demons?

Qualified for Kingdom Work

I believe there are at least four qualifications for demonstrating authority over rulers and authorities in the spiritual realm.

- BELIEF
  — Why is confidence an important component of belief? (See Ephesians 1:9.)

  — What belief is fundamental to breaking the bondage of Satan? And why is that belief crucial?

- HUMILITY
  — How do you define *humility*?

  — In whom or what do we place our confidence when we want to exercise our authority over Satan? (See John 15:5.)

  — How did Jesus model authority?

- BOLDNESS
  — How do you define *boldness*? Who serves as an example of boldness for you?

— How can knowledge lead to increased boldness?

— Turn to Revelation 21:6-8. What fate awaits the cowardly?

• DEPENDENCE
  — The authority over Satan that we have in Christ is essential for carrying out our ministry. According to the text, when are we to exercise our authority? And on whom are we to depend when we do so?

  — When is the only time we aren't to submit to the authority of government, work, home, and church?

Free from Fear

• When we boldly and humbly exercise the authority that Christ has conferred on us over the spiritual realm, we experience the freedom we all have in Christ.

  — Think back on your own life. When have you experienced freedom from fear, and how do you relate this to your exercise of your authority in Christ?

  — Look at John 8:31,32. How does this add to your understanding of your freedom in Christ?

• What step can you take today to clarify your perspective on the power of Jesus Christ over Satan? Perhaps it will mean reviewing this chapter, looking at the Gospel accounts of how Jesus operated against the powers of darkness, or fully depending upon God for direction and insight. Remember, we have no authority or power in the flesh. Satan can't do anything about our position in Christ, but if he can get us to believe it isn't true we will live as though it's not.

— Close with a prayer of thanksgiving for the authority and power you, a believer, have in Christ Jesus.

Jesus Has You Covered

CHAPTER 6

Identifying the Source

- Frances asked, "How can I tell if my problems are in my mind, or the result of sin and disobedience against God, or the evidence of demonic influence?"

  — What about Frances' letter (pages 91,92) is a clue that her problem was the result of demonic influence?

  — What realization helped Frances walk free?

God's Protection

- What is Satan's role in the life of nonbelievers? (See 2 Corinthians 4:3,4.)

- What is the deceiver's approach when a person turns his or her life over to God?

- What do the germs in our world illustrate about how demons work and how we should deal with them?

- What is the basis of our protection as Christians?

- Passivity makes us vulnerable to attacks by Satan. Ephesians 6:10-18 outlines the protection that believers have in the Lord and makes it clear that the believer should not be passive. List the commands in verses 10-13 which demand action on our part.

Dressed for Battle

- According to Ephesians 6:14-17, what does the active-duty believer wear for protection?

- What does Romans 13:14 teach about what we are actually doing when we put on this armor?

- What protection does this armor—this putting on of Christ—provide? (Look at John 14:30 and 1 John 5:18 for some additional thoughts about this.)

Armor You Have Already Put On

- Look closely at Ephesians 6:14,15. Which pieces of armor did you put on when you first received Jesus Christ as Lord and Savior?

- THE BELT OF TRUTH
  — Why is this piece of armor important in the battle against Satan? (Consider how Jesus refers to Satan in John 8:44.)

  — Give two or three specific ways in which you can practice standing firm in the truth.

- THE BREASTPLATE OF RIGHTEOUSNESS
  — What does a breastplate do?

  — What then does the breastplate of righteousness do?

  — Standing firm in righteousness involves understanding and applying the principle of confession. How is confession different from saying "I'm sorry" or asking forgiveness? Why does Satan interfere with confession?

  — What verses can you claim when Satan plants seeds of doubt about your salvation and whether God can or will forgive you?

— What does confession do in our lives?

• THE SHOES OF PEACE
    — According to Romans 5:1, when we are justified by our
      faith we have peace with God. Why is peace with fellow
      believers important as well?

    — Why would Satan be pleased with a lack of peace and
      unity among the children of God?

    — What should be the basis for peace among believers?

The Rest of the Armor
• THE SHIELD OF FAITH

    — Turn to Luke 4:1-13. How does Jesus deal with the
      devil's temptations?

    — How are believers today to deal with the doubts, temp-
      tations, and accusations which Satan sends our way?

    — How are you enlarging your shield of faith?

- THE HELMET OF SALVATION
  — Why is it important that a Christian's head be protected?

  — How does understanding our place in Christ help us to stand when under attack?

  — What Scriptures are especially powerful reminders that our salvation is secure for eternity?

- THE SWORD OF THE SPIRIT (the written Word of God and the only offensive weapon mentioned here)

  — What are two common misconceptions about Satan?

  — Why is it important to speak out loud against Satan?

  — What kinds of statements from the Word of God are effective for resisting Satan? List three or four examples.

  — What should our attitude of heart be when dealing with a satanic attack?

The Protective Power of Prayer

- The passage on Ephesians that we have been looking at ends with the command to pray. Why is prayer important for taking a stand against Satan?

- What instructions and information about prayer do the following verses give?

  — Ephesians 6:18

  — Romans 8:26

  — Philippians 4:6

- Take a few moments now to consider your prayer life. What is your attitude toward God in it? How regular is it? Is the time you spend *speaking* balanced by time spent *listening*? How expectant and confident are your prayers? Write out a specific step you will take this week to improve your prayer life.

Praying for Spiritual Sight

- What role can prayer play in the lives of people who have not yet recognized Jesus as Lord? Write out a two or three-sentence evangelistic prayer that you can pray regularly.

• How can the spiritual sight of believers be improved? Again, write out a brief prayer that you can use for yourself and fellow believers.

Binding the Strong Man

• According to Jesus' teaching in Matthew 12:29, what is the first step toward helping people become free of spiritual blindness and demonic influence?

• Summarize C. Fred Dickason's guidelines for how to pray for a person being harassed by demons.

Taking Inventory

• What aspect of your spiritual armor needs "polishing"? Write out a plan for doing just that.

• What were the two or three most striking things you learned about Satan and his ways in this chapter?

— What did you learn about Christ and His provision to help you oppose Satan?

• What perspective on evangelism has this chapter taught or reminded you about?

- How has this chapter helped you renew your commitment to prayer? What goal(s) have you set for yourself?

- Look again at the larger scriptural context of the armor of God (Ephesians 6:10-21). What do you see as the foundation(s) for our use of the armor of God in our spiritual struggle?

Part Two

Stand Firm!

Manipulating Spirits

CHAPTER 7

Sharon's Story

• What was the approach the church that specialized in spiritual warfare took in trying to help Sharon?

— What was the problem with this approach?

• Turn in your Bible to Isaiah 8:19,20. What does this Scripture tell us as God's people about dealing with spirits?

The Rebel Authority

• What action enabled Satan to take authority over the world—authority which he claimed in Luke 4:6?

• What action changed the authority Satan had? Who now has the ultimate authority over heaven as well as earth? (See Matthew 28:18.)

- When we received Christ, we became citizens of heaven (Philippians 3:20). Satan is the ruler of this world, but he is no longer *our* ruler, for Christ is our ruler. How does the Holy Spirit help us as we live on earth, Satan's turf? (See John 16:13.)

- What is the difference between influence and ownership? Explain what Satan can and cannot do to believers.

The Powers That Be

- Satan is a created being. He is not omnipresent, omniscient, or omnipotent. What do these facts about Satan suggest in regard to whether his emissaries—demons—exist?

- Consider the "two equal and opposite errors" of disbelief and "unhealthy interest" in demons of which C. S. Lewis writes. How can we counter these errors with the truth in our daily walk?

The Personality of Demons

- Luke 11:24-26 offers the following insights into the personality and individuality of evil spirits.

  1. Demons can exist outside or inside humans.
  2. They are able to travel at will.

3. They are able to communicate.
4. Each one has a separate identity.
5. They are able to remember and make plans.
6. They are able to evaluate and make decisions.
7. They are able to combine forces.
8. They vary in degrees of wickedness.

— Which of these traits was new to you?

— How does this list of characteristics influence your perspective on demons? Do they seem more or less frightening? Why?

• According to Irenaeus, why don't believers need to fear Satan?

• According to what you know about the Bible and God's promises to His children, why don't believers need to fear Satan?

Running the Gauntlet of Evil

Even when we walk in the light of Jesus Christ, evil spirits can interfere with our lives. Right now, think about your own walk down the street of row houses toward Jesus Christ. What have the beings inhabiting those houses been calling out to you?

- "Hey, look over here! I've got something you really want. It tastes good, feels good, and is a lot more fun than your boring walk down the street. Come on in and take a look."

  — What temptations are you most vulnerable to?

  — How can God's Word help you stand strong? Write out a specific verse.

- "Who do you think you are? God doesn't love you. You will never amount to anything. Surely you don't believe that bit about being saved." "See what you did! How can you call yourself a Christian when you behave like that?"

  — What accusations are particularly defeating for you?

  — Write out a specific verse from God's Word as a response to each of the accusations you listed. (Consulting the list on pages 43–45 may help.)

- "You don't need to go to church today. It's not important to pray and read the Bible every day. Some of the New Age stuff isn't so bad."

  — Where does Satan try to deceive you about your walk with the Lord?

— What commands or encouragement from the Bible can keep you walking the walk you're called to?

• In general, how does Satan try to make you slow down, stop, sit down, and even give up your journey toward Christ?

• Why is Satan's influence (and he does indeed have the ability to influence believers) potentially dangerous to Christians?

• Having looked more closely at how Satan works, why do you think it is critical that Christians know the Bible?

• How did Paul the apostle experience his "birthright" as a child of God? (See Romans 7:25–8:17.)

Running the Race

• The text outlines three ways to respond to the demonic taunts and barbs being thrown at you from those second-story windows during your daily walk with Christ (see pages 120,121).

— Which two ways are wrong?

— Why are they wrong? More specifically, how do these actions conflict with what Scripture teaches?

• What is the correct way to respond to harassment by demons?

• What practical commands in Colossians 2:6,7 and 3:1-4 can keep you walking the road toward Christ?

A Postscript

• What, if anything, in this chapter did you find disturbing? Take time to review the passage in the book that was unsettling and then open your Bible to see how it answers your questions. Share your concerns with someone you trust and whose biblical understanding you respect. Do whatever is necessary to put your questions to rest so that Satan and his demons won't find a foothold of doubt in your mind.

• What statements in this chapter were especially encouraging to you? Make a note of those that help provide the strength and courage you need to stand strong in Christ Jesus.

The Lure of
Knowledge and Power

CHAPTER 8

A Trap As Old As the Bible

• What is often the lure of the occult?

• With what are we to satisfy our God-given desire for knowledge?

• Look again at Moses' command to the children of Israel in Deuteronomy 18:9-13.

— Where do you see parallels with our world today?

— What can or should a Christian do in this situation?

65

— What does the information from our survey (see page 126) indicate about the appeal of the occult to Christians? About Christians' ignorance of the dangers of the occult?

Knowledge from the Dark Side

• Why do you think words from a psychic or a channeler are more appealing to people than what God has to say?

• What do you think Satan is doing through today's psychics, channelers, palm-readers, card-readers, and other New Age practitioners? What is Satan's ultimate goal?

Charlatans and Real Mediums

• Where do charlatans and real mediums get the information they share?

• What differing goals do charlatans and real mediums have?

• What is a believer's best defense against whatever appeal these fortune-tellers may have?

The Down Side of Seeking the Dark Side

• How is the relationship between God's Spirit and Old Testament kings Saul and David different from the relationship between God's Spirit and New Testament believers today?

• What do the following verses say about a believer's security?

— Ephesians 1:13,14

— John 10:28

— Romans 8:35-39

• According to 1 Samuel 16:14, "the Spirit of the Lord departed from Saul, and an evil spirit from the Lord terrorized him." Why would God send an evil spirit to a person or nation?

• What caused the evil spirit to leave Saul temporarily? (See 1 Samuel 16:23.)

• What does this passage from Samuel suggest about the prominence of music in the spiritual realm?

• What are the source and the impact of much of today's popular secular music?

• What warning is inherent in these facts?

• Look again at the story of the rich man and Lazarus in Luke 16:19-31.

— What does this story teach about the possibility of the living communicating with the dead?

— In light of this teaching, how are believers to regard psychics who claim contact with the dead, psychologists who claim to regress a client back to a former existence, and New Age mediums who purport to channel a person from the past into the present?

An Old Idea in New Clothing

• How is Satan the deceiver at work in the New Age movement? Consider some of the New Age watchwords and catchphrases.

- How is today's New Age situation similar to the times of the early church and even the world of our Hebrew ancestors?

  — Acts 8:9,10

  — Acts 16:16-18

  — Leviticus 17:7

  — Psalm 106:36-38

  — Deuteronomy 32:15-18

  — 1 Timothy 4:1

- Even believers are vulnerable to being lured away by the counterfeit knowledge and power of our enemy, who exaggerates our sense of independence and importance apart from God. How can we, who are God's children, protect ourselves in this area?

A Postscript

- What, if anything, in this chapter did you find disturbing? Take time to review the passage in the book which was unsettling and then open your Bible to see how it answers your questions. Share your concerns with someone you trust and whose biblical understanding you respect. Do whatever is necessary to put your questions to rest so that Satan and his demons won't find a foothold of doubt in your mind.

- What statements in this chapter were especially encouraging? Make a note of those which help provide the strength and courage you need to stand strong in Christ Jesus.

Tempted to Do It Your Way

CHAPTER 9

Temptation and Sin

- Does the fact that a person is bombarded by tempting thoughts mean that he or she is a sinner? Why or why not?

- How is sin different from temptation?

- Does temptation automatically lead to sin? Explain your answer.

— Read Hebrews 4:16. What resource do we have in time of temptation?

- Write out the promise of 1 Corinthians 10:13 and memorize this powerful verse.

The Basis of Temptation

- What characterizes the life of a person who is spiritually dead?

- According to the text, what are we tempted to look to in order to meet our basic needs?

— Why is this so?

- Read Philippians 4:19. What does this verse teach about what God will do for His people?

- What determines the power of temptation in a person's life?

Too Much of a Good Thing

- How do you define *sin*?

• Look again at the good which can become sin.

Physical rest	becomes	laziness
Quietness	becomes	noncommunication
The ability to profit	becomes	avarice and greed
Enjoyment of life	becomes	intemperance
Physical pleasure	becomes	sensuality
Interest in the possessions of others	becomes	covetousness
Enjoyment of food	becomes	gluttony
Self-care	becomes	selfishness
Self-respect	becomes	conceit
Communication	becomes	gossip
Cautiousness	becomes	unbelief
Positiveness	becomes	insensitivity
Anger	becomes	rage and bad temper
Lovingkindness	becomes	overprotection
Judgment	becomes	criticism
Same-sex friendship	becomes	homosexuality
Sexual freedom	becomes	immorality
Conscientiousness	becomes	perfectionism
Generosity	becomes	wastefulness
Self-protection	becomes	dishonesty
Carefulness	becomes	fear

— Which items on this list warn you of potential areas of sin in your life?

— Take those areas of concern before the Lord in prayer right now.

• What new understanding of sin do this list and the discussion on pages 136–138 offer you?

Sin Versus Growth

• Turn in your Bible to 1 John 2. According to verses 12-14, what characterizes the following three stages of Christian growth?

— "Little children"

— "Young men"

— "Fathers"

• Which stage are you in right now?

• What are you doing to ensure your continuing growth in Christ?

Channels of Temptation

- According to 1 John 2:16, what are the three channels through which Satan will entice you to act independently of God?

- Describe the three channels of temptation you just listed.

The Lust of the Flesh

- Satan watched Jesus fast for 40 days and concluded that His hunger might be a point of vulnerability. What other soft spots of vulnerability does Satan look for in believers?

- In Matthew 4:1-11, Jesus modeled a way of resisting Satan's temptations, whatever channel he chooses. Jesus countered the temptations with the Word of God—the source of life we can draw on for strength. What truth did Jesus claim in Matthew 4:4 in response to Satan's appeal to the lust of the flesh?

The Lust of the Eyes

- How can the things we see weaken our confidence in God?

- What is wrong and dangerous about a "prove it to me" attitude?

• What truth did Jesus claim in Matthew 4:7?

The Pride of Life

• How does the New Age movement espouse the pride of life?

• How did Satan use the pride of life to become the god of this world?

• Satan offered Jesus the kingdom of the world just as he had offered it to Adam and Eve. In response, what truth did Jesus claim in Matthew 4:10?

*There are three critical issues reflected in these channels of temptation we have just looked at: 1) the **will of God,** as expressed through your **dependence on God;** 2) the **Word of God,** as expressed through **your confidence in God;** and 3) the **worship of God,** as expressed through your humble **obedience to God.** Be aware!*

Two of Our Biggest Appetites

• Temptation's hook is the devil's guarantee that what we think we want and need outside God's will can satisfy us. In reality, what is the only thing that can truly satisfy our heart's desires?

- *Eat to Live or Live to Eat?* Food is necessary for survival and basic physical health. What are some unnatural reasons people turn to food? Do you find yourself turning to food for any of those reasons? If so, consider the spiritual dimension of that action and take your struggle to the Lord in prayer.

- *Sexual Passions Unleashed.* Sex is a natural, God-given part of life, but it is also a powerful temptation to sin. Why is sexual sin unique and uniquely dangerous? See Romans 6:12,13 and 1 Corinthians 6:18. If Satan is using sex to tempt you to stray from God and the path He calls you to, remember to address the spiritual dimension of that temptation.

The Way of Escape

- Turn to 2 Corinthians 10:5 and look at the second part of that verse. What is the first step for escaping temptation when a tempting thought enters your mind?

- The second step for standing strong against temptation is to evaluate the thought which Satan has planted in your mind. Turn to Philippians 4:8. List the eightfold criterion for what believers should think about.

- What should a believer do with a thought which fails the test of God's Word, a thought which doesn't meet the standards listed in Philippians 4:8?

- Confession and resisting the devil comprise an important step of escape. What does James 4:7 promise about the effectiveness of this step?

- Think about what you've learned about Satan. How can you better resist sin when the devil plants tempting thoughts in your mind?

Submit, Confess, Resist, Change

- Read James 4:6-8 and 1 John 2:1. Who and what are our resources for changing, so that we can break the "sin-confess-sin-confess" cycle?

A Postscript

- Was anything in this chapter disturbing to you? Do whatever is necessary to put your questions to rest so that Satan and his demons won't find a foothold of doubt in your mind.

- What statements in this chapter were especially encouraging to you? Make a note of those which help provide the strength and courage you need to stand strong in Christ Jesus.

Accused by the Father of Lies

CHAPTER 10

Satan's Accusations

• Why are accusations effective weapons in Satan's battle against the kingdom of God? In other words, what do accusations keep believers from doing?

• Why are accusations a powerful follow-up to the temptations that believers give in to?

• What accusations does Satan frequently use against you?

• Write out a verse from Scripture to counter each one of those lies.

Putting the Accuser in His Place

Zechariah 3:1-10 shows how God responds to our accuser. This teaches us an important truth about how we can stand strong against Satan's accusations.

The Lord Rebukes Satan

• In this scene, what is Satan doing?

• What does God say in response to Satan's words?

• Imagine an earthly parallel to this courtroom scene. How can you effectively respond to Satan's accusing words?

The Lord Removes Our Filthy Garments

• Why are Satan's accusations groundless? Think about the cross of Christ.

• Who removes our unrighteousness?

• Why is it important to remember that we in ourselves don't have any garments of righteousness to put on that will satisfy God?

The Lord Admonishes Us to Respond

• God rebukes Satan and clothes us in righteousness. How does He want us to respond? (See Zechariah 3:7.)

• What are some practical ways you can walk in God's ways, serve Him, and live out your identity in Christ? Be specific.

Recognizing a Critical Difference

• The devil's accusations and the Holy Spirit's convictions both cause sorrow, but that sorrow moves us in two different directions. Where do Satan's accusations lead? And where do the Holy Spirit's convictions lead?

• How can you determine whether you are being falsely accused? What feelings and thoughts about yourself will you have if Satan is the one causing your sorrow?

• What truth about sorrow do you see illustrated in the contrasting life-stories of Judas Iscariot and Simon Peter?

• Read the following verses and compare the work of Satan and Jesus Christ.

— Revelation 12:10. The work of Satan:_____

— Hebrews 7:25. The work of Jesus: _____

_____

The Quicksand of Accusation

• What can happen if we refuse to take a stand against the accuser?

• Satan will tell believers lies about their worth. We are to ignore those lies and instead believe what God says about us. What does God say about you? Write out the following Scriptures, plus any others you think of. These words of truth are words of freedom which can keep you from sinking in the quicksand of Satan's accusations.

— Romans 5:8

— 1 John 3:1

— Psalm 139

— 1 John 1:9

— Romans 8:38,39

— Someone is against us, but it can't be God. Why not?

—Who will bring a charge against God's elect? It can't be God. Why not?

—Who is the one who condemns? It can't be Jesus. Why not?

—Who can separate you from the love of God?

The Unpardonable Sin

• What are the sources of a believer's fear that he or she has committed the unpardonable sin?

— Which piece of our spiritual armor does this fear weaken?

• Look again at Mark 3:22-30. How do we know from Jesus' teaching that a believer cannot commit the unpardonable sin?

• The devil can mislead us, discourage us, and accuse us of something we've never even done. What might our questioning of "authorities" be, since we know that it cannot be blasphemy of the Holy Spirit? (See 1 John 4:1-6.)

A Postscript

• Was anything in this chapter disturbing to you? Do whatever is necessary to put your questions to rest so that Satan and his demons won't find a foothold of doubt in your mind.

• What statements in this chapter were especially encouraging? Make a note of those which help provide the strength and courage you need to stand strong in Christ Jesus.

The Danger of Deception

CHAPTER 11

Satan's Number-One Strategy

• Satan will attempt to dissuade believers through self-deception, false prophets/teachers, and deceiving spirits. What aspects of your spiritual armor need to be ready to do battle?

Beware of Self-Deception

The Scriptures reveal several patterns of behavior through which Christians become vulnerable to self-deception.

• We deceive ourselves when we hear the Word of God but don't do it.

— What are we commanded in James 1:22 and 2:14-20?

— If you are a preacher or teacher, does your life always measure up to the passage of Scripture you are sharing? What does or should this inconsistency compel you to do?

— When you receive the Word through another person's teaching, do you faithfully put it into practice? Why or why not?

— What should a believer's life model instead of perfectionism?

— Why would honesty in a Christian community—honesty about struggles, failures, and sins—discourage Satan and his demons?

• We deceive ourselves when we say we have no sin.

— What does Romans 3:23 teach about sinfulness?

— What does 1 John 1:8 add to that teaching?

— Why is it important to confess and deal with sin on a daily basis?

- We deceive ourselves when we think we are something we are not.

  — By what, and whose, standards should we believers evaluate ourselves?

  — What cautions do Romans 12:3 and Galatians 6:3 offer?

  — Who is the source of all your goodness? Who then should receive the credit for any goodness in you?

- We deceive ourselves when we think we are wise in this age.

  — What do the following verses teach about real wisdom?

  1 Corinthians 2:16

  1 Corinthians 3:18,19

  Proverbs 3:5,6

  Job 42:1,2

  Psalm 111:10

— Think about today's world. Where does the "wisdom" of the world reflect immoral, ungodly, and humanistic values? List several examples.

— How do you keep yourself standing strong in God's values?

• We deceive ourselves when we think we are religious but do not bridle our tongue.

— What does Scripture teach about the power of the tongue?

James 1:26

Luke 6:45

Ephesians 4:29

James 3:5-12

Proverbs 10:19

— How then does our tongue reflect our devotion or lack of devotion to God?

• We deceive ourselves when we think we will not reap what
we sow.

— What can result from the seeds we sow in this life?

Galatians 6:7-10

Proverbs 22:8

Hosea 10:12,13

2 Corinthians 9:6

Luke 6:38

— God forgives our sins, but He doesn't necessarily spare
us from the consequences of those sinful acts. When did
God teach you this lesson? Be specific.

• We deceive ourselves when we think the unrighteous will
inherit the kingdom of God.

— What does 1 Corinthians 6:9,10 teach about who will
not inherit the kingdom of God?

— What does James 2:14-19,22,26 teach about how a
believer's life should reflect his or her faith?

- We deceive ourselves when we think we can continually associate with bad company and not be corrupted.

  — What do Proverbs 22:24,25 and 1 Corinthians 15:33 teach about the importance of the company we keep?

  — When have you seen the truth of this teaching in your own life or the life of someone you care about?

  — Do these biblical teachings prohibit ministry to the amoral or immoral people of the world? Explain.

Beware of False Prophets and Teachers

- Compare the counterfeit with the real.

  — Criterion #1: As the Old Testament prophets modeled, what effect do the words of true prophecy have on those who hear them? (See Jeremiah 23:22.)

  — Criterion #2: What is the ultimate authority guiding a true prophet's message? (See Jeremiah 23:25-28.)

— Criterion #3: What is the effect of a prophecy from the Lord? (See Jeremiah 23:29.)

— Criterion #4: What phrase can tip you off to an act of plagiarism by a so-called prophet? Why wouldn't God use a person in this way?

• Test signs and wonders.

— What guideline does Deuteronomy 18:22 offer?

— Now look at Deuteronomy 13:1-3, Matthew 24:23-25, and Mark 13:22. What is the purpose of false signs and wonders?

— An occurrence of the miraculous does not necessarily mean the presence of God. What can a believer do to test all signs, wonders, and dreams?

• Beware of counterfeits in the church.

— In his second epistle, Peter warns about false prophets and teachers who operate within the church. What will they do? (See 2 Peter 2:1.)

— Although the biblical criteria for evaluating ministry are truth and righteousness, how will false teachers in the church lead you to evaluate their ministry? (See 2 Peter 2:2 and page 176 of the text.)

— What are two characteristics of false prophets? (See 2 Peter 2:10.)

— How do the leadership roles outlined in Scripture prevent false teachers from arising? How closely does your church follow those biblical teachings on church leadership?

Beware of Deceiving Spirits

• What warnings do the following Scriptures offer?

—1 Timothy 4:1

— 1 John 2:18

— 1 John 4:1-6

• What did Hannah Whitehall Smith's perspective on pages 177, 178 of the text teach you about demons?

• What major points should be contained in a prayer for freedom from deceiving spirits? (An example is given on page 178.)

Spiritual Discernment

• What is the pure motive for true spiritual discernment?

• Spiritual discernment is not a mere function of the mind. What is discernment a function of? Explain.

• Why is discernment an important gift to individual believers and to the church in general?

• Why are we more vulnerable to Satan's deception than to his temptations or accusations?

• What is the only effective weapon against the darkness of Satan's deception?

A Postscript

• Was anything in this chapter disturbing to you? Do whatever is necessary to put your questions to rest so that Satan and his demons won't find a foothold of doubt in your mind.

• What statements in this chapter were especially encouraging? Make a note of those which help provide the strength and courage you need to stand strong in Christ Jesus.

The Danger of Losing Control

CHAPTER 12

Spiritual Vulnerability

• Satanic intrusion does not mean satanic ownership. How does Romans 8:35-39 support this truth?

• Even though he can never own a believer, how does Satan seem to control a believer's life?

Kingdoms in Conflict

• Some Christians argue that believers cannot yield control to evil spirits. What things suggest that this argument is incorrect?

• Why does the English term "demon-possessed" sometimes lead to confusion?

• In what way is our vulnerability a "matter of degree"?

Saints in Bondage

• If we don't accept the reality that Christians can come under demonic influence, we will likely blame ourselves or God for the problems we face. What is the problem with blaming ourselves or God?

Scripture supports the fact that believers can lose control or come under bondage to demons, as the following passages illustrate.

• Luke 13:10-17. Note where the woman was (verse 10) and how she was described (verse 16). What things didn't protect her from Satan's power?

• Luke 22:31-34. What request did Satan make of Jesus? And what does the fact that Satan made the request suggest about a believer's vulnerability?

- Ephesians 6:10-17. What does the existence of this armor and the command to put it on suggest about the power and strategy of demons?

- James 3:14-16. What warning does James offer believers?

- 1 Timothy 4:1-3. Who will be "paying attention to deceitful spirits and doctrines of demons"?

- 1 Corinthians 5:1-13. What suggests that the man discussed in this passage was a believer?

- Ephesians 4:26,27. According to this passage, what is one way believers can give Satan a foothold in their lives?

- 1 Peter 5:6-9. What are two other ways that believers can give Satan a foothold?

- Acts 5:1-11. What does the story of Ananias and Sapphira teach you about the possibility and consequences of Satan's control of believers?

The Devil Did Not Make You Do It

When you allow Satan to deceive you in any area of your life, you are vulnerable to his control in that area.

- What is inaccurate about the phrase "The devil made me do it"?

- How is a person's free will or choice involved in the devil's control of his or her life?

- What is—and what is not—at stake if you allow Satan to control an area of your life?

- On what does God's protection of believers depend? Asked another way, how do we as believers activate the protection God promises?

- What acts of responsibility in putting on our spiritual protection are outlined for each believer in these now-familiar passages? (See also page 185 in the text.)

— Romans 13:14

— 2 Corinthians 10:15

— Romans 6:12

— James 4:7

- In the letter titled "Silence," the woman who wrote it describes some specific steps of responsibility she took in her life. List two or three of these steps that you see her take in the letter, and then list some Scripture verses that relate to those actions. How do you think you can follow her in the path of responsibility?

A Postscript

- Was anything in this chapter disturbing to you? Do whatever is necessary to put your questions to rest so that Satan and his demons won't find a foothold of doubt in your mind.

- What statements in this chapter were especially encouraging? Make a note of those which help provide the strength and courage you need to stand strong in Christ Jesus.

Part Three

Walk Free!

Steps to
Freedom in Christ

CHAPTER 13

Freedom in Christ

- Evaluate your daily walk with the Lord.

  — Have you lost a measure of your freedom in Christ because you have disobeyed God?

  — What do you need to do to make right your relationship with God?

- Now remind yourself about the real issue.

  — What are the Steps, in a nutshell?

— What is it only God can do, which is also at the heart of the Steps?

If you have lost your freedom in Christ, it is because of what you have chosen to believe and do. Consequently, your freedom will be the result of now choosing to believe the truth, resist the devil, and submit to God.

Step 1: Counterfeit vs. Real

Renounce your past or present involvements with occult practices and cult teachings and rituals, as well as non-Christian religions.

• Complete the "Non-Christian Spiritual Checklist" on pages 202–204 of the text. If you don't have the book, ask God to help you list all your involvements with occult practices and cult teachings and rituals, as well as non-Christian religions.

• Pray the following prayer:

> Dear heavenly Father, I ask You to bring to my mind anything and everything that I have done knowingly or unknowingly that involves occult, cult, or non-Christian teachings or practices. I want to experience Your freedom by renouncing these things right now. In Jesus' name I pray. Amen.

• Go through the additional questions on page 204 (if you have the text) and write down everything God brings to mind. Use a separate sheet of paper.

• Once you have completed your checklist and the questions, confess and renounce *each* item you were involved in by praying the following prayer *out loud:*

Lord, I confess that I have participated in_____. I
know it was evil and offensive in Your sight. Thank You for
Your forgiveness. I renounce any and all involvement with
_____, and I cancel out any and all ground that the
enemy has gained in my life through this activity. In Jesus'
name, amen.

Renouncing Wrong Priorities

Confront your wrong priorities.

• Who were we created to worship?

• What do we as believers know in addition to this? (See 1 John
  5:20.)

• What can idols be, besides stone or wooden images?

• Complete the checklist on pages 206,207 of the text. If
  you don't have the text, ask God to help you list, as com-
  pletely as possible, the areas where things or people have
  become more important to you than the true God, Jesus
  Christ.

• Use the following prayer to renounce any areas of idolatry
  or wrong priority the Holy Spirit brings to your mind.

In the name of the true and living God, Jesus Christ, I
renounce my worship of the false god of (name the idol). I

choose to worship only You, Lord. I ask You, Father, to enable me to keep this area of (<u>name the idol</u>) in its proper place in my life.

Special Renunciations for Satanic Ritual Involvement

- If you have been involved in satanic rituals or heavy occult activity (or you suspect it because of blocked memories, severe and recurring nightmares, or sexual bondage or dysfunction), I strongly urge you to say out loud the "Special Renunciations for Satanic Ritual Involvement" on page 208. (If you don't have the text, I also urge you to obtain it for this purpose.) Read across the page, renouncing the first item in the column under "Domain of Darkness" and then announcing the first truth in the column under "Kingdom of Light." Continue down the page in that manner.

- Keep in mind that you may need special counseling from someone who understands spiritual conflicts if you have suffered from abuse during satanic involvement.

Step 2: Deception vs. Truth

Accept and believe the truth of God's Word in the innermost part of your being. Lay aside falsehood and deception.

- Look at John 14:6, 16:13, and 17:17; and Ephesians 4:14-16.

  — What do these verses say about truth in regard to the persons of the Godhead?

— What specifically does Ephesians 4:14-16 say about truth in relationships?

• In Psalm 32:2, what did David write about living without deceit?

— What do you think "blessed" would mean to you in your experience of the walk of truth?

• Where does the strength to "walk in the light" (1 John 1:7) come from?

• Pray the following prayer:

> Dear heavenly Father, I know that You want me to know the truth, believe the truth, speak the truth, and live in accordance with the truth. Thank You that it is the truth that will set me free. In many ways I have been deceived by Satan, the father of lies, and I have deceived myself as well.
>
> Father, I pray in the name of the Lord Jesus Christ, by virtue of His shed blood and resurrection, asking You to rebuke all of Satan's demons that are deceiving me.
>
> I have trusted in Jesus alone to save me, and so I am Your forgiven child. Therefore, since You accept me just as I am in Christ, I can be free to face my sin and not try to hide. I ask for the Holy Spirit to guide me into all truth. I ask You to "search me, O God, and know my heart; try me and know my anxious thoughts; and see if there be any hurtful way in me, and lead

me in the everlasting way." In the name of Jesus, who is the
Truth, I pray. Amen.

(See Psalm 139:23,24.)

- As you go through the checklist titled "Ways you can be deceived by the world" on pages 211,212 and list areas that apply to your life, take the time to look up the Scriptures and think about them. Whether or not you have the text available, pray to God that He would bring to your memory those things you need to put down in this area.

- Pray this prayer of confession:

> Lord, I confess that I have been deceived by _____.
> I thank You for Your forgiveness, and I commit myself to
> believing only Your truth. In Jesus' name, amen.

- Work through the checklist titled "Ways to deceive yourself" on pages 212,213. Again, if you don't have the text, write down these kind of deceptions as God brings them to mind. Take the time to look up the Scriptures and think about them.

- Pray this prayer of confession for each deception you need to renounce:

> Lord, I confess that I have deceived myself by _____.
> Thank You for Your forgiveness. I commit myself to believing
> only Your truth. In Jesus' name, amen.

- Complete the checklist of "Ways to wrongly defend yourself" on page 213. If the text is not available to you, place your dependence in God to help you put down things that are necessary for you to confess.

- Use this prayer to confess these sins:

> Lord, I confess that I have defended myself wrongly by_____. Thank You for Your forgiveness. I now commit myself to trusting in You to defend and protect me. In Jesus' name, amen.

- What do we need to learn about the lies we have used to defend ourselves?

- What must we recognize about faith?

- If you have found that your relationship with God the Father is hindered by your past experiences, read your way *out loud* through the lists on page 217. (I strongly recommend that you obtain the text for this.)

- Fear can only control us if we let it. In order to begin to experience freedom from the bondage of fear and the ability to walk by faith in God, pray the following prayer from your heart:

> Dear heavenly Father, I confess to You that I have listened to the devil's roar and have allowed fear to master me. I have not always walked by faith in You but instead have focused on my feelings and circumstances. Thank You for forgiving me for my unbelief. Right now I renounce the spirit of fear and affirm the truth that You have not given me a spirit of fear but of power, love, and a sound mind. Lord, please reveal to my mind now all the fears that have been controlling me so I can renounce them and be free to walk by faith in You.
>
> I thank You for the freedom You give me to walk by faith and not by fear. In Jesus' powerful name, I pray. Amen.
>
> (See 2 Corinthians 4:16-18; 5:7; 2 Timothy 1:7.)

- Use the checklist on page 217 as a guide to identifying fears in your life. Write down as many areas as God enables you to, even if you don't have the text available to guide you.

- Follow this by renouncing each fear specifically, using this prayer:

> I renounce the (name the fear) because God has not given me a spirit of fear. I choose to live by faith in the God who has promised to protect me and meet all my needs as I walk by faith in Him.
>
> (See Psalm 27:1;
> Matthew 6:33,34; 2 Timothy 1:7.)

- Sum up your dealing with fear by praying this:

> Dear heavenly Father, I thank You that You are trustworthy. I choose to believe You, even when my feelings and circumstances tell me to fear. You have told me not to fear, for You are with me; to not anxiously look about me, for You are my God. You will strengthen me, help me, and surely uphold me with Your righteous right hand. I pray this with faith in the name of Jesus my Master. Amen.
>
> (See Isaiah 41:10.)

- Fear stands opposed to faith, and true faith must be grounded in the truth.

— What must our response be to truth?

— How has the New Age movement twisted the idea of faith?

- Read aloud the following "Statement of Truth." You may find it very helpful to read it daily for several weeks to renew your mind with the truth and replace any lies you may be believing.

Statement of Truth

1. I recognize that there is only one true and living God who exists as the Father, Son, and Holy Spirit. He is worthy of all honor, praise, and glory as the One who made all things and holds all things together. (See Exodus 20:2,3; Colossians 1:16,17.)

2. I recognize that Jesus Christ is the Messiah, the Word who became flesh and dwelt among us. I believe that He came to destroy the works of the devil, and that He disarmed the rulers and authorities and made a public display of them, having triumphed over them. (See John 1:1,14; Colossians 2:15; 1 John 3:8.)

3. I believe that God demonstrated His own love for me in that while I was still a sinner, Christ died for me. I believe that He has delivered me from the domain of darkness and transferred me to His kingdom, and in Him I have redemption, the forgiveness of sins. (See Romans 5:8; Colossians 1:13,14.)

4. I believe that I am now a child of God and that I am seated with Christ in the heavenlies. I believe that I was saved by the grace of God through faith, and that it was a gift and not a result of any works on my part. (See Ephesians 2:6,8,9; 1 John 3:1-3.)

5. I choose to be strong in the Lord and in the strength of His might. I put no confidence in the flesh, for the weapons of warfare are not of the flesh but are divinely powerful for the destruction of strongholds. I put on the full armor of God. I resolve to stand firm in my faith and resist the evil one. (See 2 Corinthians 10:4; Ephesians 6:10-20; Philippians 3:3.)

6. I believe that apart from Christ I can do nothing, so I declare my complete dependence on Him. I choose to abide in Christ in order to bear much fruit and glorify my Father. I announce to Satan that Jesus is my Lord. I reject any and all counterfeit gifts or works of Satan in my life. (See John 15:5,8; 1 Corinthians 12:3.)

7. I believe that the truth will set me free and that Jesus is the truth. If He sets me free, I will be free indeed. I recognize that walking in the light is the only path of true fellowship with God and man. Therefore, I stand against all of Satan's deception by taking every thought captive in obedience to Christ. I declare that the Bible is the only authoritative standard for truth and life. (See John 8:32,36; 14:6; 2 Corinthians 10:5; 2 Timothy 3:15-17; 1 John 1:3-7.)

8. I choose to present my body to God as a living and holy sacrifice and the members of my body as instruments of righteousness. I choose to renew my mind by the living Word of God in order that I may prove that the will of God is good, acceptable, and perfect. I put off the old self with its evil practices and put on the new self. I declare myself to be a new creation in Christ. (See Romans 6:13; 12:2; 2 Corinthians 5:17 NIV; Colossians 3:9,10.)

9. By faith, I choose to be filled with the Spirit so that I can be guided into all truth. I choose to walk by the Spirit so that I will not carry out the desires of the flesh. (See John 16:13; Galatians 5:16; Ephesians 5:18.)

10. I renounce all selfish goals and choose the ultimate goal of love. I choose to obey the two greatest commandments: to love the Lord my God with all my heart, soul, mind, and strength and to love my neighbor as myself. (See Matthew 22:37-39; 1 Timothy 1:5.)

11. I believe that the Lord Jesus has all authority in heaven and on earth, and He is the head over all rule and authority. I

am complete in Him. I believe that Satan and his demons are subject to me in Christ since I am a member of Christ's body. Therefore, I obey the command to submit to God and resist the devil, and I command Satan in the name of Jesus Christ to leave my presence. (See Matthew 28:18; Ephesians 1:19-23; Colossians 2:10; James 4:7.)

Step 3: Bitterness vs. Forgiveness

Forgive others as you have been forgiven for your sin through Jesus' death on the cross (Ephesians 4:31,32).

• Ask God to bring to your mind the people you need to forgive by praying the following prayer out loud:

> Dear heavenly Father, I thank You for the riches of Your kindness, forbearance, and patience toward me, knowing that Your kindness has led me to repentance. I confess that I have not shown that same kindness and patience toward those who have hurt me. Instead, I have held on to my anger, bitterness, and resentment toward them. Please bring to my mind all the people I need to forgive in order that I may do so now. In Jesus' name, amen.
>
> (See Romans 2:4.)

• On a separate sheet of paper, list the names of people who come to your mind. At this point don't question whether you need to forgive them or not. If a name comes to mind, just write it down.

Often we hold things against ourselves as well, punishing ourselves for wrong choices we've made in the past. Write "myself" at the bottom of your list so you can forgive yourself.

Also write down "thoughts against God" at the bottom of your list. Obviously, God has never done anything wrong so we don't have to forgive Him. Sometimes, however, we harbor angry thoughts against Him because He did not do what we wanted Him to do. Those feelings of anger or resentment against God can become a wall between us and Him, so we must let them go.

• What does forgetting have to do with forgiving?

• Is forgiveness a matter of the will or of the emotions? Explain.

— What does holding on to the right to revenge do to us?

— How is forgiveness an act of trust in God?

• How does a person who forgives benefit from that act?

— Do we benefit from forgiveness even if we have to keep living with the consequences of someone else's sin? Explain.

• How do our emotions play both a positive and negative role in forgiveness?

• Work through your list of people to forgive. Starting with the first person on your list, make the choice to forgive him or her for every painful memory that comes to your mind. Stay with that individual until you are sure you have dealt with all the remembered pain. Then work your way down the list in the same way.

As you begin forgiving people, God may bring to your mind painful memories you've totally forgotten. Let Him do this even if it hurts. God wants you to be free; forgiving those people is the only way. Don't try to excuse the offender's behavior, even if it is someone you are really close to.

Don't say, "Lord, please help me to forgive." He is already helping you and will be with you all the way through the process. Don't say "Lord, I want to forgive…" because that bypasses the hard choice we have to make. Say, "Lord, I *choose* to forgive…."

• For every painful memory you have for each person on your list, pray out loud:

> Lord, I choose to forgive (name the person) for (what the person did) even though it made me feel (share the painful feelings).

• After you have forgiven each person for all the offenses that came to your mind, and after you have honestly expressed how you felt, conclude your forgiveness of that person by praying out loud:

> Lord, I choose not to hold onto my resentment. I thank You for setting me free from the bondage of my bitterness. I relinquish my right to seek revenge and ask You to heal my damaged emotions. I now ask You to bless those who have hurt me. In Jesus' name, I pray. Amen.

Step 4: Rebellion vs. Submission

It is easy to believe the lie that those in authority over us are only robbing us of the freedom to do what we want. The truth is that God has placed them there for our protection and liberty. Rebelling against God and the authorities He has set up is a very serious sin, for it gives Satan a wide-open avenue to attack. Submission is the only solution. God requires more, however, than just the outward appearance of submission; He wants us to sincerely submit from the heart to those in authority. When you stand under the authority of God and those He has placed over you, you cut off this dangerous opening for demonic attacks.

• What are our biblical responsibilities in regard to authority?

• What do the following passages teach about submission to authority?

— Romans 13:1-5

— 1 Timothy 2:1-4

— 1 Peter 2:13-16

— 1 Peter 2:18-21

— 1 Peter 3:1,2

— Ephesians 6:1-3

— Hebrews 13:17

• How is submission to human authority an act of faith?

• What is the only exception to the biblical command to submit to human authority? (See Acts 4:19 and 5:29.)

• Pray as you look over the list on pages 227,228. Look up the Scriptures you haven't already thought upon, and list the specific ways in which you have been rebellious towards authority. Ask God to help you remember the things you need to write down, even if you don't have a copy of the text.

• Use the following prayer to specifically confess these sins:

> Lord, I confess that I have been rebellious toward (<u>name</u>) by (<u>say what you did specifically</u>). Thank You for forgiving my rebellion. I choose now to be submissive and obedient to Your Word. In Jesus' name, I pray. Amen.

Step 5: Pride vs. Humility

Let go of pride which says, "I don't need God or anyone else," and humble yourself before your heavenly Father and sovereign Lord.

• Why is pride so deadly to one's spiritual life?

- According to Philippians 3:3, what is a good definition of humility?

- What instructions do the following passages give?

  — James 4:6-10

  — 1 Peter 5:1-10

- Use the following prayer to express your commitment to living humbly before God:

> Dear heavenly Father, You have said that pride goes before destruction and an arrogant spirit before stumbling. I confess that I have been thinking mainly of myself and not of others. I have not denied myself, picked up my cross daily, and followed You. As a result, I have given ground to the devil in my life. I have sinned by believing I could be happy and successful on my own. I confess that I have placed my will before Yours, and I have centered my life around myself instead of You.
>
> I repent of my pride and selfishness and pray that all ground gained in my members by the enemies of the Lord Jesus Christ would be canceled. I choose to rely on the Holy Spirit's power and guidance so I will do nothing from selfishness or empty conceit. With humility of mind, I will regard others as more important than myself. And I choose to make You, Lord, the most important of all in my life.
>
> Please show me now all the specific ways in which I have lived my life in pride. Enable me through love to serve others and in honor to prefer others. I ask all of this in the gentle and humble name of Jesus, my Lord. Amen.
>
> (See Proverbs 16:18; Matthew 6:33; 16:24; Romans 12:10; Philippians 2:3.)

- Having made this commitment in prayer, now allow Him to show you any specific ways in which you have lived in a proud manner, using the list on pages 230,231. If you don't have the text, do your best to be as complete as God enables you to be.

- For each of these areas that has been true in your life, pray out loud:

> Lord, I agree I have been proud in (name the area). Thank You for forgiving me for my pride. I choose to humble myself before You and others. I choose to place all my confidence in You and none in my flesh. In Jesus' name, I pray. Amen.

Dealing with Prejudice and Bigotry

Pride sets one person or group against another. Satan's strategy is always to divide and conquer, but God has given us a ministry of reconciliation.

- Turn to 2 Corinthians 5:16-21. What is the basis for our personal ministry of reconciliation?

— How does our position in Christ wipe out any cause or motive for prejudice and bigotry?

- Consider your own heart as you ask God in prayer to reveal areas of proud prejudice:

> Dear heavenly Father, I know that You love all people equally and that You do not show favoritism. You accept people from every nation who fear You and do what is right. You do not judge them based on skin color, race, economic

> standing, ethnic background, gender, denominational pref-
> erence, or any other worldly matter. I confess that I have too
> often prejudged others or regarded myself as superior
> because of these things. I have not always been a minister of
> reconciliation but have been a proud agent of division
> through my attitudes, words, and deeds. I repent of all hateful
> bigotry and proud prejudice, and I ask You, Lord, to now reveal
> to my mind all the specific ways in which this form of pride
> has corrupted my heart and mind. In Jesus' name, amen.

- For each area of prejudice, superiority, or bigotry that the
  Lord brings to mind, pray the following prayer out loud
  from your heart:

> I confess and renounce the prideful sin of prejudice
> against (name the group). I thank You for Your forgiveness,
> Lord, and ask now that You would change my heart and make
> me a loving agent of reconciliation with (name the group). In
> Jesus' name, amen.

Step 6: Bondage vs. Freedom

To find freedom from the vicious cycle of "sin-confess-
sin-confess," we must follow James 4:7 by submitting to God
and resisting the devil.

- How can other believers help you if you feel trapped by
  habitual sin? (See James 5:16.)

- Whom can you call on to pray for and with you? Do so.

- How can you be sure God will forgive you for your sin? Write out the promise of 1 John 1:9, and replace the *we, us,* and *our* with *I, me,* and *my.*

- Pray the following prayer out loud:

> Dear heavenly Father, You have told me to put on the Lord Jesus Christ and make no provision for the flesh in regard to its lusts. I confess that I have given in to fleshly lusts that wage war against my soul. I thank You that in Christ my sins are already forgiven, but I have broken Your holy law and given the devil a chance to wage war in my body. I come to You now to confess and renounce these sins of the flesh so that I might be cleansed and set free from the bondage of sin. Please reveal to my mind now all the sins of the flesh I have committed and the ways I have grieved the Holy Spirit. In Jesus' holy name, I pray. Amen.
>
> (See Proverbs 28:13 NIV; Romans 6:12,13; 13:14; 2 Corinthians 4:2; James 4:1; 1 Peter 2:5-8,11.)

- There are many sins of the flesh that can control us. You may want to open your Bible to Galatians 5:19-21, Ephesians 4:25-31, and Mark 7:20-27 and pray through these verses, asking the Lord to reveal the ways you have specifically sinned. Use the checklist on page 234 as well, if you have the text available, to make as complete record as possible of those things you need to confess.

- Confess each of these sins specifically by praying:

> Lord, I confess that I have committed the sin of (name the sin). Thank You for Your forgiveness and cleansing. I now turn away from this sin and turn to You, Lord. Strengthen me by Your Holy Spirit to obey You. In Jesus' name, amen.

- It is our responsibility to not allow sin to have control over our bodies. We must not use our bodies or another person's body as an instrument of unrighteousness (Romans 6:12,13).

- From 1 Corinthians 6:15-20, give two reasons why sexual immorality is an especially serious matter.

- Dwell on these verses as you allow God to bring to your mind those sexual sins you must gain freedom from. Pray this prayer:

  > Lord, I ask You to bring to my mind every sexual use of my body as an instrument of unrighteousness so I can renounce these sins right now. In Jesus' name, I pray. Amen.

- As the Lord brings to your mind every wrong sexual use of your body, whether it was done to you (rape, incest, sexual molestation) or willingly by you (pornography, masturbation, sexual immorality), renounce *every* occasion:

  > Lord, I renounce (<u>name the specific use of your body</u>) with (<u>name any other person involved</u>). I ask You to break that sinful bond with (<u>name</u>).

- After you are finished, commit your body to the Lord by praying:

  > Lord, I renounce all these uses of my body as an instrument of unrighteousness, and I admit to any willful participation. I choose now to present my eyes, mouth, mind, heart, hands, feet, and sexual organs to You as instruments of righteousness. I present my whole body to You as a living sacrifice, holy and acceptable. I choose to reserve the sexual use of my body for marriage only.

I reject the devil's lie that my body is not clean or that it is dirty or in any way unacceptable to You as a result of my past sexual experiences. Lord, thank You that You have totally cleansed and forgiven me and that You love and accept me just the way I am; therefore, I choose now to accept myself and my body as clean in Your eyes. Amen.

(See Hebrews 13:4.)

Special Prayers for Special Needs

o If the Lord has brought to your mind a special need, use one of these special prayers to confess your sin, renounce deception, and claim your freedom in Christ in that area.

Divorce

Lord, I confess to You any part that I played in my divorce (ask the Lord to show you specifics). Thank You for Your forgiveness, and I choose to forgive myself as well. I renounce the lie that my identity is now in "being divorced." I am a child of God, and I reject the lie that says I am a second-class Christian because of the divorce. I reject the lie that says I am worthless, unlovable, and that my life is empty and meaningless. I am complete in Christ who loves me and accepts me just as I am. Lord, I commit the healing of all hurts in my life to You as I have chosen to forgive those who have hurt me. I also place my future into Your hands and trust You to provide the human companionship You created me to need through Your church and, if it be Your will, through another spouse. I pray all this in the healing name of Jesus, my Savior, Lord, and closest friend. Amen.

Homosexuality

Lord, I renounce the lie that You have created me or anyone else to be homosexual, and I agree that in Your Word You clearly forbid homosexual behavior. I choose to accept myself as a child of God, and I thank You that You created me as a man (woman). I renounce all homosexual thoughts, urges, drives, and acts, and cancel out all ways that Satan has used these things to pervert my relationships. I announce that I am free in Christ to relate to the opposite sex and my own sex in the way that You intended. In Jesus' name, amen.

Abortion

Lord, I confess that I was not a proper guardian and keeper of the life You entrusted to me, and I admit that as sin. Thank You that because of Your forgiveness, I can forgive myself. I recognize the child is in Your caring hands for all eternity. In Jesus' name, amen.

Suicidal Tendencies

Lord, I renounce all suicidal thoughts and any attempts I've made to take my own life or in any way injure myself. I renounce the lie that life is hopeless and that I can find peace and freedom by taking my own life. Satan is a thief and comes to steal, kill, and destroy. I choose life in Christ who said He came to give me life and give it abundantly. Thank You for Your forgiveness that allows me to forgive myself. I choose to believe that there is always hope in Christ. In Jesus' name, I pray. Amen.

(See John 10:10.)

Drivenness and Perfectionism

Lord, I renounce the lie that my self-worth is dependent upon my ability to perform. I announce the truth that my identity and sense of worth is found in who I am as Your child. I renounce seeking the approval and acceptance of other people, and I choose to believe that I am already approved and accepted in Christ because of His death and resurrection for me. I choose to believe the truth that I have been saved, not by deeds done in righteousness, but according to Your mercy. I choose to believe that I am no longer under the curse of the law because Christ became a curse for me. I receive the free gift of life in Christ and choose to abide in Him. I renounce striving for perfection by living under the law. By Your grace, heavenly Father, I choose from this day forward to walk by faith in the power of Your Holy Spirit according to what You have said is true. In Jesus' name, amen.

Eating Disorders or Self-Mutilation

Lord, I renounce the lie that my value as a person is dependent upon my appearance or performance. I renounce cutting or abusing myself, vomiting, using laxatives or starving myself as a means of being in control, altering my appearance, or trying to cleanse myself of evil. I announce that only the blood of the Lord Jesus cleanses me from sin. I realize I have been bought with a price and my body, the temple of the Holy Spirit, belongs to God. Therefore, I choose to glorify God in my body. I renounce the lie that I am evil or that any part of my body is evil. Thank You that You accept me just the way I am in Christ. In Jesus' name, I pray. Amen.

Substance Abuse

Lord, I confess that I have misused substances (alcohol, tobacco, food, prescription or street drugs) for the purpose of pleasure, to escape reality, or to cope with difficult problems. I confess that I have abused my body and programmed my mind in a harmful way. I have quenched the Holy Spirit as well. Thank You for forgiving me. I renounce any satanic connection or influence in my life through my misuse of food or chemicals. I cast my anxieties on to Christ who loves me. I commit myself to yield no longer to substance abuse, but instead I choose to allow the Holy Spirit to direct and empower me. In Jesus' name, amen.

• After you have confessed all known sin, pray:

Lord, I now confess these sins to You and claim through the blood of the Lord Jesus Christ my forgiveness and cleansing. I cancel out all ground that evil spirits have gained through my willful involvement in sin. I pray this in the wonderful name of my Lord and Savior, Jesus Christ. Amen.

Step 7: Curses vs. Blessings

The next step to freedom is to renounce the sins of your ancestors as well as any curses that may have been placed on you by deceived and evil people or groups.

- Exodus 20:4-6 deals with the need for this step. How would you describe that need?

- What conditions can contribute toward causing someone to struggle with a particular sin?

- Ask the Lord to show you specifically what sins are characteristic of your family by praying the following prayer:

  > Dear heavenly Father, I ask You to reveal to my mind now all the sins of my ancestors that are being passed down through family lines. I want to be free from those influences and walk in my new identity as a child of God. In Jesus' name, amen.

- As the Lord brings those areas of family sin to your mind, list them on a separate sheet of paper.

- In order to walk free from the sins of your ancestors and any curses and assignments targeted against you, read the following declaration and pray the following prayer out loud.

Declaration

I here and now reject and disown all the sins of my ancestors. I specifically renounce the sins of (list here the areas of family sin the Lord revealed to you). As one who has now been delivered from the domain of darkness into the kingdom of God's Son, I cancel out all demonic working that has been passed down to me from my family. As one who has been crucified and raised with Jesus Christ and who sits with Him in heavenly places, I renounce all satanic assignments that are directed toward me and my ministry. I cancel out every curse that Satan and his workers have put on me. I announce to Satan and all his forces that Christ became a curse for me when He died for my sins on the cross. I reject any and every way in which Satan may claim ownership of me. I belong to the Lord Jesus Christ who purchased me with His own blood. I reject all blood sacrifices whereby Satan may claim ownership of me. I declare myself to be fully and eternally signed over and committed to the Lord Jesus Christ. By the authority I have in Christ, I now command every familiar spirit and every enemy of the Lord Jesus that is influencing me to leave my presence. I commit myself to my heavenly Father to do His will from this day forward.

(See Galatians 3:13.)

Prayer

Dear heavenly Father, I come to You as Your child, bought out of slavery to sin by the blood of the Lord Jesus Christ. You are the Lord of the universe and the Lord of my life. I submit my body to You as an instrument of righteousness, a living and holy sacrifice that I may glorify You in my body. I now ask You to fill me with the Holy Spirit. I commit myself to the renewing of my mind in order to prove that Your will is good, acceptable, and perfect for me. All this I pray in the name and authority of the risen Lord Jesus Christ. Amen.

Maintaining Your Freedom

• What things can we do to maintain the freedom we have gained?

• Upon whom must we always depend for our freedom?

• Freedom will be yours as long as you keep choosing the truth and standing firm in the strength of the Lord. Some people have found it helpful to walk through the "Steps to Freedom in Christ" again. To maintain your freedom in Christ, I strongly suggest the following as well:

1. Be involved in a loving, caring church fellowship where you can be open and honest with others and where God's truth is taught with grace.

2. Read and meditate on the Bible daily. Memorize key verses from the "Steps to Freedom in Christ." You may want to read the "Statement of Truth" (see Step 2) out loud daily and study the verses mentioned.

3. Learn to take every thought captive to the obedience of Christ. Assume responsibility for your thought life. Don't let your mind become passive. Reject all lies, choose to focus on the truth, and stand firm in your true identity as a child of God in Christ.

4. Don't drift back to old patterns of thinking, feeling, and acting. This can happen very easily if you become spiritually and mentally lazy. If you are struggling with walking in the truth, share your battles openly with a trusted friend who will pray for you and encourage you to stand firm.

5. Don't expect other people to fight your battles for you, however. They can help you, but they can't think, pray, read the Bible, or choose the truth for you.

6. Commit yourself to daily prayer. Prayer demonstrates a life of trusting in and depending on God. You can pray the following prayers often and with confidence.

Let the words come from your heart as well as your lips and feel free to change them to make them *your* prayers.

Daily Prayer and Declaration

Dear heavenly Father, I praise You and honor You as my Lord. You are in control of all things. I thank You that You are always with me and will never leave me nor forsake me. You are the only all-powerful and only wise God. You are kind and loving in all Your ways. I love You and thank You that I am united with Christ and spiritually alive in Him. I choose not to love the world or the things in the world, and I crucify the flesh and all its passions.

Thank You for the life I now have in Christ. I ask You to fill me with the Holy Spirit so I may say no to sin and yes to You. I declare my total dependence upon You and I take my stand against Satan and all his lying ways. I choose to believe the truth of God's Word despite what my feelings may say. I refuse to be discouraged; You are the God of all hope. Nothing is too difficult for You. I am confident that You will supply all my needs as I seek to live according to Your Word. I thank You that I can be content and live a responsible life through Christ who strengthens me.

I now take my stand against Satan and command him and all his evil spirits to depart from me. I choose to put on the full armor of God so I may be able to stand firm against all the devil's schemes. I submit my body as a living and holy sacrifice to God, and I choose to renew my mind by the living Word of God. By so doing I will be able to prove that the will of God is good, acceptable, and perfect for me. In the name of my Lord and Savior, Jesus Christ. Amen.

Bedtime Prayer

Thank You, Lord, that You have brought me into Your family and have blessed me with every spiritual blessing in the heavenly places in Christ Jesus. Thank You for this time of renewal and refreshment through sleep. I accept it as one of Your blessings for Your children, and I trust You to guard my mind and my body during my sleep.

As I have thought about You and Your truth during the day, I choose to let those good thoughts continue in my mind while I am asleep. I commit myself to You for Your protection against every attempt of Satan and his demons to attack me during sleep. Guard my mind from nightmares. I renounce all fear and cast every anxiety upon You, Lord. I commit myself to You as my rock, my fortress, and my strong tower. May Your peace be upon this place of rest now. In the strong name of the Lord Jesus Christ, I pray. Amen.

Prayer for Cleansing Home/Apartment/Room

After removing and destroying all objects of false worship, pray this prayer aloud in every room if necessary:

Heavenly Father, I acknowledge that You are the Lord of heaven and earth. In Your sovereign power and love, You have given me all things to enjoy. Thank You for this place to live. I claim my home as a place of spiritual safety for me and my family, and ask for Your protection from all the attacks of the enemy. As a child of God, raised up and seated with Christ in the heavenly places, I command every evil spirit claiming ground in this place, based on the activities of past or present occupants including me, to leave and never return. I renounce all curses and spells directed against this place. I ask You, heavenly Father, to post Your holy, warring angels around this place to guard it from any and all attempts of the enemy to enter and disturb Your purposes for me and my family. I thank You, Lord, for doing this in the name of the Lord Jesus Christ. Amen.

Prayer for Living in a Non-Christian Environment

After removing and destroying all objects of false worship from your possession, pray this aloud in the place where you live:

Thank You, heavenly Father, for a place to live and to be renewed by sleep. I ask You to set aside my room (or portion of this room) as a place of spiritual safety for me. I renounce any allegiance given to false gods or spirits by other occupants. I renounce any claim to this room (space) by Satan based on the activities of past or present occupants, including me. On the basis of my position as a child of God and joint-heir with Christ, who has all authority in heaven and on earth, I command all evil spirits to leave this place and never return. I ask You, heavenly Father, to station Your holy, warring angels to protect me while I live here. In Jesus' mighty name, I pray. Amen.

- Continue to walk in the truth that your identity and sense of worth comes through who you are in Christ. Renew your mind with the truth that your *acceptance, security,* and *significance* are in Christ alone.

In Christ

- Use the affirmations from Scripture on pages 248–250 (if you have the text available) to continue renouncing lies and maintaining your freedom.

  — I suggest reading each of the Scripture verses out loud. Spend some time thinking about what they have come to mean to you.

  — As you go through the affirmations, put your own name in each sentence and read it out loud. These affirmations are truth from God for you to receive and believe.

- Spend a few moments thanking God for the freedom that is yours through Jesus Christ.

Seeking Forgiveness

• Read Matthew 5:23-26. Who or what is it that helps us remember the wrongs we have done to others?

• Which principles do we need to follow in deciding whether our wrongs require us to go to another person to ask forgiveness?

• As God brings to mind those people whose forgiveness you need to seek, use the step-by-step process on pages 251, 252 to direct you. (I suggest you obtain the text for this purpose.)

Helping Others Find Freedom in Christ

CHAPTER 14

The Truth Shall Set You Free

- What is *not* required to help people find freedom from bondage to Satan?

- What *is* required to help people find freedom from bondage to Satan?

Principles of Spiritual Conflict Resolution

- How does the illustration of the house help us see the real issues in resolving spiritual conflicts?

- What must we keep in mind about God's role in our work with other people?

I would like to suggest the following four principles as we consider the spiritual side of conflict resolution.

• *Principle 1:* We should derive our methodology for dealing with the kingdom of darkness primarily from the epistles rather than the Gospels and the Book of Acts.

— What significant event happened between the events of the Gospels and the writing of the epistles? Be specific.

— Why then do the epistles offer better guidelines for us believers living after the cross and Pentecost?

• *Principle 2:* Just because there are no instructions in the epistles to cast out demons does not mean that Christians cannot have spiritual problems. It means that the responsibility for living free in Christ has shifted from the specially endowed agent of authority to the individual believer.

— The epistles *do* contain instructions for *individual* believers, including individuals who are in bondage to Satan. Why are instructions to those individuals—to people who are being counseled—more important than instructions to the counselors?

— What is the essence of the ministry of helping people find freedom in Christ?

— In helping people find their freedom in Christ, what course of action should we take in dealing with demons?

• *Principle 3:* Dealing with the demonic should be seen as a truth encounter rather than a power encounter.

— Satan deals with lies, power, and darkness. How can a Christian effectively confront the lies and deception of Satan?

— Take another look at Ephesians 1:18,19. What should our attitude be in regard to power and authority?

— Why does Satan try to make his victim fearful?

— How are we to glorify God in our encounters with Satan's influence?

• *Principle 4:* The primary prerequisites for helping others find freedom are godly character and the ability to teach.

— According to 2 Timothy 2:24-26, what are the qualifications for helping others find freedom?

— Why is teaching an important aspect of helping people find freedom from Satan's bondage?

— In any helping situation, on whom should the helper be totally dependent? Why?

— What are the specific advantages of a "truth encounter"?

Guidelines for Helping People Find Freedom

• What normal counseling skills are important to helping people find freedom?

Keep in mind the skills you just listed as you think through the following guidelines for helping people find freedom.

1. Gather Background Information

— What tools are available for this?

— Why is thorough background information crucial to the process?

— What are some important things to learn about the family of the person you're counseling?

— What is important for you to learn about the person? (Remember to learn about all aspects of his or her life.)

2. Determine False Beliefs

— Most people in spiritual conflict have a distorted concept of God and of themselves. What causes a distorted concept of God?

— In what way are people often blocked from a true concept of God?

— What characterizes the false self-concept of many people in bondage?

— Why is a believer's false concept of the "two kingdoms" another effective arena for Satan's attacks?

— What is the truth about God's position and Satan's position?

3. Deal with the Individual, Not the Demons

— As you work with people in bondage to Satan, why is it important to have them share what is going on in their minds?

— Look at the prayer recommended to begin a session (page 200 of the text). What are the major points covered?

— How must the person being counseled cooperate during a session? Why is this important?

— Why shouldn't you touch the person you're counseling during a session?

— If the person you're counseling is experiencing intense internal struggle or is experiencing opposition that is too great, what basic and critical facts must you return to?

4. Lead Them Through the Steps to Freedom

— On pages 266,267 I make several points from my experience in helping people to freedom. Try to list two or three of these in your own words.

— In which steps will you likely find that the person you are helping will experience the most opposition?

— Why is this so?

— Why do you think it is important to exhort the people you have counseled to stand firm in the Lord and to work to maintain their freedom?

A Final Encouragement

We Can Win the War

- In what respect has the victory over Satan already been won?

- What must Christians do to appropriate that victory? Be specific.

- Ask God to guide your ministry to those who are in bondage to Satan. May He bless you as you help people in bondage reach out to the Bondage Breaker, Jesus Christ.

> *Indeed, the Lord will comfort Zion;*
> *He will comfort all her waste places.*
> *And her wilderness he will make like Eden,*
> *And her desert like the garden of the Lord;*
> *Joy and gladness will be found in her,*
> *Thanksgiving and sound of a melody.*
> *—Isaiah 51:3*

Books and Resources from
Neil T. Anderson,
Discipleship Counseling Ministries,
and Freedom in Christ Ministries

Core Message and Resources

- *The Bondage Breaker®* (Harvest House). Study guide and audiobook also available. This book explains spiritual warfare, what your protection is, ways that you are vulnerable, and how you can live a liberated life in Christ. Well over 1 million copies in print.

- *Victory Over the Darkness* with study guide, audio book, and videos (Regal Books). Explains who you are in Christ, how you walk by faith, how your mind and emotions function, and how to relate to one another in Christ. Well over 1 million copies in print.

- *Breaking Through to Spiritual Maturity* (Regal Books). A curriculum for teaching the basic message of Discipleship Counseling Ministries.

- *Discipleship Counseling* with videos (Regal Books). Discipleship and counseling are integrated practically with theology and psychology to help Christians resolve personal and spiritual conflicts through repentance and faith in God.

- *Steps to Freedom in Christ* and interactive video (Regal Books). This discipleship counseling tool helps Christians resolve their personal and spiritual conflicts.

- *Beta, The Next Step in Discipleship* (Gospel Light). A 12-lesson course for Sunday school classes and small groups, designed to enable new and stagnant believers to resolve personal and spiritual conflicts and be established alive and free in Christ. Includes teacher's guide, student guide, and two DVDs.

- *The Daily Discipler* (Regal books). A five-day-per-week one-year study to thoroughly ground the believer in their faith. Based on Neil's books; covers the major doctrines of the Christian faith and the problems Christians face.

The Bondage Breaker® Series (Harvest House). Truth from the Word of God on specific issues—to bring you help and freedom in your life.

- *Praying by the Power of the Spirit*
- *Finding Freedom in a Sex-Obsessed World*

Resources on Specific Issues

- *Getting Anger Under Control* with Rich Miller (Harvest House). Exposes the basis for anger and shows how you can control it.

- *Freedom from Fear* with Rich Miller (Harvest House). Discusses fear, anxiety, and anxiety disorders and reveals how you can be free from them.

- *Daily in Christ* (Harvest House). This popular daily devotional will encourage, motivate, and challenge you to experience the reality of *Christ in you.*
- *Breaking the Bondage of Legalism* with Rich Miller and Paul Travis (Harvest House). An exposure and explanation of legalism, the guilt and shame it brings, and how you can overcome it.
- *God's Power at Work in You* with Dr. Robert Saucy (Harvest House). A thorough analysis of sanctification, along with practical instruction on how you can grow in Christ.
- *A Way of Escape* (Harvest House). Exposes the bondage of sexual strongholds and shows you how they can be torn down in Christ.
- *Who I Am in Christ* (Regal Books). 36 short chapters on who you are in Christ and how He meets your deepest needs.
- *Freedom from Addiction* with Mike Quarles (Regal Books).
- *One Day at a Time* with Mike Quarles (Regal Books).
- *The Christ-Centered Marriage* with Dr. Charles Mylander (Regal Books).
- *The Spiritual Protection of Our Children* with Peter and Sue Vander Hook (Regal Books).
- *Leading Teens to Freedom in Christ* with Rich Miller (Regal Books).
- *Finding Hope Again* with Hal Baumchen (Regal Books). Depression and how to overcome it.
- *Freedom in Christ Bible* (Zondervan). A one-year discipleship study with notes in the Bible.
- *Blessed Are the Peacemakers* with Dr. Charles Mylander (Regal Books).
- *A Biblical Guide to Alternative Medicine* with Dr. Michael Jacobson (Regal Books).
- *Setting Your Church Free* with Dr. Charles Mylander (Regal Books).
- *Christ-Centered Therapy* with Dr. Terry and Julie Zuehlke (Zondervan).
- *Released from Bondage* with Judy King and Dr. Fernando Garzon (Thomas Nelson).

The Victory Over the Darkness Series (Regal Books)
- *Overcoming a Negative Self-Image* with Dave Park
- *Overcoming Addictive Behavior* with Mike Quarles
- *Overcoming Doubt*
- *Overcoming Depression*

Youth Books

- *The Bondage Breaker® Youth Edition* with Dave Park (Harvest House)
- *Stomping Out the Darkness* with Dave Park (Regal Books)
- *Stomping Out Depression* with Dave Park (Regal Books)

To order the material listed above, please contact the following:

In the USA:

Freedom in Christ Ministries
9051 Executive Park Drive, Suite 503
Knoxville, TN 37923
Telephone: (865) 342-4000
E-mail: info@ficm.org
Web site: www.ficm.org

e3 Partners Ministry
317 Main Street, Suite 207
Franklin, TN 37064
Telephone: (888) 354-9411
Web site: www.e3partners.org

In Canada:

FIC Canada
Box 33115
Regina, SK S4T7X2
Canada
Telephone: (306) 546-2522
E-mail: FreedominChrist@sasktel.net

In the United Kingdom:

Freedom in Christ Ministries UK
P.O. Box 2842
Reading, UK RG29RT
Telephone: (118) 988-8173
E-mail: info@ficm.org.uk

To order youth editions of Dr. Anderson's books coauthored by Dave Park contact:

His Passion Ministries
PO Box 23495
Knoxville, TN 37933-1495
Telephone: (865) 966-1153
E-mail: davepark@tds.net
Web site: www.hispassionministries.com